English for Meetings

Phrases, Expressions, and One Case to Be Fluent in Meetings

ADAMA KOMOU

Also by the Author

ENGLISH FOR CONSULTANTS: Expressions, Phrases, and Cases to Be an Effective Team Player

Copyright © 2020 by Adama Komou

All rights reserved.

No part of this book can be reproduced in any form or by any electronic or mechanical means, including information storage and retrieval systems, without permission in writing from the publisher, except by a reviewer who may cite brief passages in a review.

ENGLISH FOR MEETINGS: Phrases, Expressions, and One Case to Be Fluent in Meetings

Design by Licorne Management Sarl
Images by ZdenekSasek on VectorStock.com

To my parents,

Nathalie and Lassina Komou.

Table of Contents

Preface vi
1. Prepare 10
2. Requesting 13
3. Open 24
4. Agree 31
5. Disagree 34
6. Interrupt 37
7. Ask Opinion 39
8. Clarify 41
9. Make a Point 43
10. Give a Reason 45
11. Report Progress 46
12. Report Regress 47
13. Moderate 48
14. Close 48
15. Exercises 52

About the Author 54
Bibliography 57

Preface

I don't have a bachelor's degree in the English language.

A couple of years ago, I was struggling to find a short and comprehensive book that would allow me to add value quickly as a non-native aspiring management consultant. I wondered why English books looked so *academic*, and if some people were feeling the same.

I had to go through many books and courses with no time available. Down the line, I came to reach a plateau. I couldn't seem to make any improvement out of my additional readings and speaking. I started putting together my English toolbox of words, expressions, ideas, and phrases to break the plateau and reach the executive English-speaking level.

Meanwhile I discovered that high-level business professionals don't *speak* English; they *compile a code of thinking*. Ever since, the whole paradigm in which I was learning shifted. I found that if you wanted to *speak* like an executive, you would first need to *crack their code of thinking*. This finding confirmed when I got into top professional environments, first in consulting, and then at the World Bank.

I thought I should share my experience to provide a *less academic* peer-to-peer way of learning executives' business English, with a shorter learning curve as well.

In this book, I am trying to give you a unique immersion in that code of thinking, using a simple layout that allows the quickest learning. In every part, you will uncover a part of the code and resolutely *be fluent in meeting*.

This is not an exhaustive book, as you will not find everything in it. However, it is a good benchmark for non-native (and native) professionals.

PREFACE

Who Is This Book For?

This book is for pre-intermediate non-native (and native) professionals who are struggling to fully deploying their talent and value in a competitive English-speaking professional environment.

This includes, but is not limited to:

- Managers
- Consultants
- Business Analysts
- HR professionals
- Marketers
- Accountants
- Engineers
- Economists
- Non-profit professionals
- Trainers
- Militaries
- Career changers
- Students

How to Benefit from This Book

When it comes to learning, we all have our learning styles. Some of us are visual learners, others are kinesthetic, and several people are auditive learners. In addition to your approach to learning, I suggest to:

PREFACE

- Make at least one cover to cover skimming
- Read regularly to recall all the ideas, words, and expressions
- Read out loud or read with your lips trying to speak out
- Always imagine a situation where you apply expressions
- Memorize a few phrases for deliberate practice
- Re-read the parts several times
- Complete exercises

Icons Used in This Book

✓ Listing
💬 Spoken expression
📄 Written expression

Fictive Names Used in This Book

ABC will stand for *"Always Be Consulting."*

Fictive company and project names include:

- ABC Consulting/Client
- ABC Project/Client
- Fintech Project / Client
- Water Project/Client
- Food Project/Client
- Health Project/Client
- Pharmaceutical Project/Client
- New Drug Project

***Important Notice

No information shared in this book is from my former/current employer nor any previous/current client.

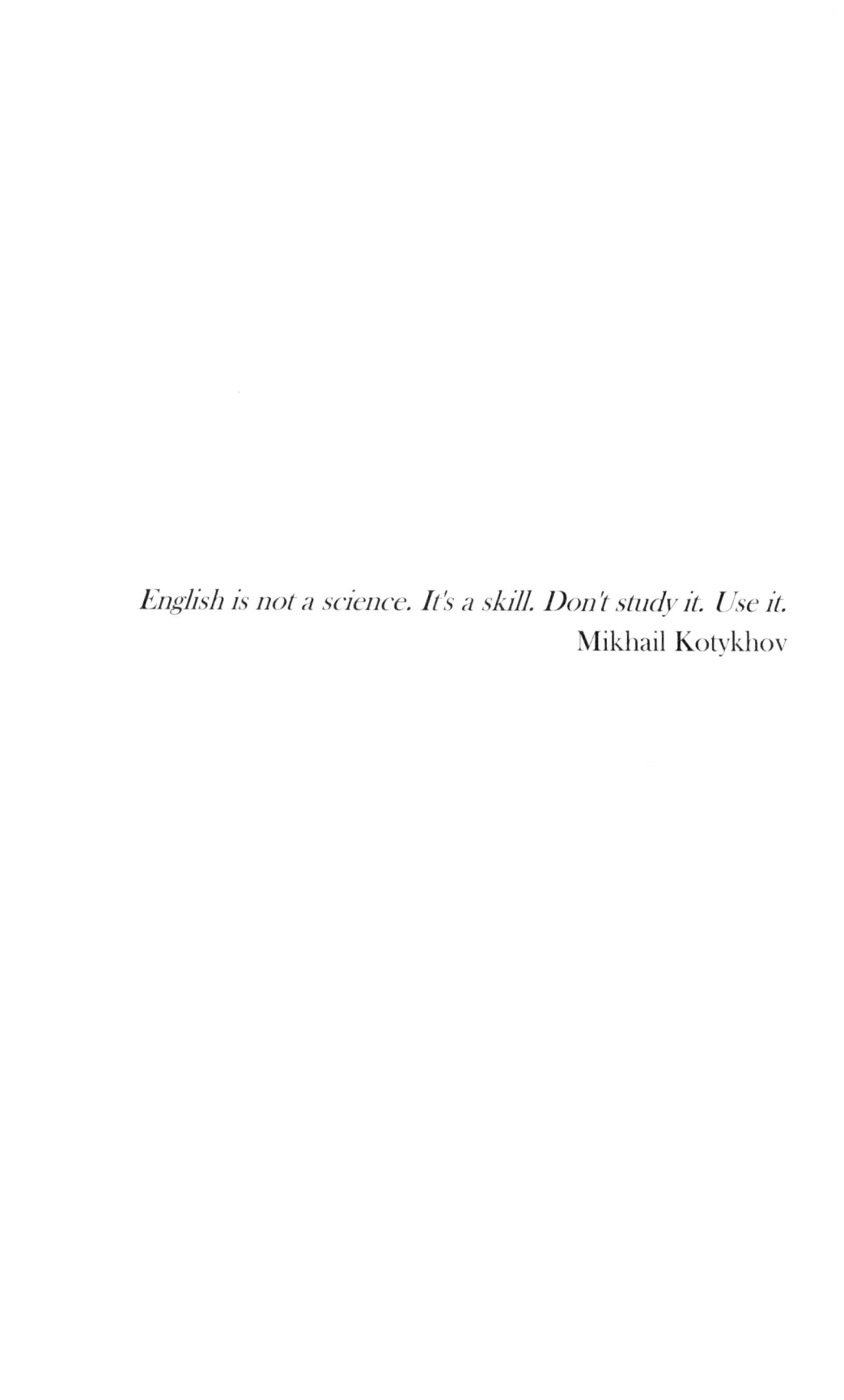

English is not a science. It's a skill. Don't study it. Use it.
Mikhail Kotykhov

1. Prepare

⇒ It's a Meeting Or:

gathering	appointment	rendezvous	reunion
assembly	session	event	consultation
encounter	date	talk	rally
convention	summit	interview	discussion

⇒ Different Types of Meeting

annual general meeting	progress meeting	decision meeting	review meeting
negotiation meeting	kickoff meeting	shareholder meeting	board meeting
team meeting	monthly meeting	weekly meeting	breakfast meeting
luncheon meeting	dinner meeting	informational meeting	workshop

ENGLISH FOR MEETINGS

brainstorming	one on one	video conferencing	group discussion
focus group	job fair	the grapevine	business luncheon
networking luncheon	work luncheon	awards luncheon	media luncheon
press luncheon	conference	symposium	seminar

⇒ Reasons for Meetings

review progress collectively	approve a proposition or project	react to changes or events	share or discuss new information
communicate efficiently	amend a document	develop options	approve plans and reports
exercise a legal responsibility	make decisions	solve problems	find and confront ideas
launch a project	raise awareness on some matters	prepare documents	validate a report

⇒ Checklist for Informal Meetings

- Date and time
- Meeting room or place
- Length
- Agenda outline

ENGLISH FOR MEETINGS

⇒ Checklist for Formal Meeting

- Terms of reference
- Meeting room and site booking
- Meeting creation in the system
- Invitation letters or emails
- Detailed agenda shared with participants
- Accounting and finance matters
- Trips and hotel management
- Procurement and vendor management
- Stationery and other furniture
- Video projector and projection screen
- Logistics and in-city transportation facilities
- Identity, rank, and origin of guests
- Welcoming of distinguished guests
- Speeches, attendance sheet, and minutes
- Coffee and lunch break services
- Dinner and cocktail services

2. Request

In Speaking

- Let's schedule a meeting for Monday to cover the details.

- Why not having a meeting tomorrow to discuss the options?

- Could we meet to go through the problem that just cropped up?

- Should we schedule a time to meet with the VC (venture capitalist)?

- Let's schedule a meeting sometime next week to discuss what can be done.

- The best thing to do is to have a meeting with Jack to set the record straight.

- Could we organize a team meeting for next Monday at the building site at 3 PM?

- Perhaps we could meet and go around all the implications of this new piece of legislation.

- I am Alan Ross from ABC Consulting, and I would like to have a meeting with you to discuss something of interest for both of us.

ENGLISH FOR MEETINGS

In Writing

📄 Hi,

Hope you are very well. I am from Bangalore and I live in Brooklyn for three years now. Please let me know if you get time to share coffee. (1)

Thank you,
Arun

📄 Hi,

Hope all is well with you. I also graduated from the London School of Economics, and I am currently working in Paris. Please let me know if you have time to share a cup of wine. (1)

Thanks a lot,
Brian

📄 Dear Colleagues,

The next monthly meeting will take place on May 15, 2019, at ABC Consulting Headquarters in Paris. The theme of the meeting will be "Knowledge Management."

I encourage you to send your Practice Improvement Note by May 05, 2019.

All the best,
Cheng

📄 Dear Robert,

I am writing to invite you to the 2nd Annual Global Operational Improvement Summit, set to take place in San Francisco on June 10th - 12th, 2018. Please find attached the event's agenda.

Here is an outline:

- Organizational improvement Scorecard
- Case study presentations
- Panel discussions
- Breakout sessions

Day two will focus exclusively on interactive workshops hosted by the Fairmont San Francisco Hotel.

ABC will also be launching its first Excellence Award Night to showcase and honor the most outstanding organizational and individual achievements through the application of the Baldrige Organizational Excellence Framework.

Yours truly,
Harry

Dear colleagues,

We would like to invite you to join the upcoming staff briefings hosted by **HR** regarding the recent International Footprint updates communicated by senior management. The presentations are open to all staff.

During the session, we will share details on several **HR** policy measures that are part of an overall effort to support the firm's international development.

The proposals mainly cover two areas – (a) how to strengthen global mobility benefits and (b) how to better facilitate global careers for staff.

This event is an early opportunity for **HR** to have your takes.

We look forward to your participation.

Best regards,
Alicia

📄 Dear colleagues,

We would like to invite you to the Decision Meeting for the ABC project. The meeting will be held on Monday, November 25, from 11:30 am to 1:00 pm UTC, in room 15 at Hong Kong with connections to Boston, New Delhi, and Johannesburg. Please see the connection details below.

Andrew Carlson (Partner, Boston), Arjun Singh (Partner, New York), and Christine Dupont (Director, Paris) will chair the meeting.

Sandra Lee (Director, London), Ashley Williams (Director, Kimberley), and Mamadou Konate (Director, Johannesburg) have kindly agreed to serve as peer reviewers.

Cordially,
Maria

📄 Dears,

As you are aware, the ABC Mediation Committee is an internal conciliation forum of first resort for the resolution of conflicts submitted by employees alleging unfair treatment or violation of employment contract terms. Its decisions are not binding.

ABC Mediation Committee will be hosting an overview of the last year's factsheets. All employees are invited to virtually attend this event, which will take place Wednesday, 7 January 2020, from 2:00 pm – 3:30 pm European Central Time. The speakers are:

- Introductory Remarks – Jacques Riviere, Executive Secretary
- Case Review Presenter – Alison Rometty, Counsel,
- Commentator – David Cheng, Senior Counsel

If possible, we ask that you share the event with your colleagues.

Those connecting through internal streaming may use the following link: http://link

Otherwise, kindly find below the Skype instructions to connect remotely.

We hope you are able to attend!

Sincerely,
Tom

Dear colleagues,

We look forward to receiving your comments on the attached package by the end of the day, Friday, December 12, 2019 ECT.

Comments may be addressed to the team copied in this email. They are seeking guidance on the following aspects:

1. Are the analytical foundations for the work solid?
2. Is the material in the document appropriately structured and accessibly written?
3. Does the project scaling plan appropriately reflect and incorporate lessons learned from the pilot stage?
4. Does the marketing plan adequately emphasize the links between pricing and segmentation, taking advantage of low hanging fruits?
5. Are the implementation arrangements and measures to coordinate project activities across various functions and cross-sectoral interests appropriately defined?

Following the efficient review process, an annotated agenda will be prepared by the project team and circulated before the meeting.

Kind regards,
Rebecca

⇒ Proposing the Time/Place for the Meeting

- Would half-past two suit you?

- How about next Monday at two?

- What time do you have in mind?

- Which day do you have in mind?

- How about sometime next week?

- What about this afternoon instead?

- Would you be available on Wednesday?

- Can I suggest that we meet at our offices?

- Are we going to meet the whole morning?

- Would Friday next week be suitable for you?

- Let say on the 1st of February in the morning.

- Could we perhaps meet next week to go over the details?

- Let's keep the length of the meeting to one hour for now.

> Let's say about one hour and a half. Is that all right for you?

> Would it be suitable to meet on June 10 at your Seattle offices to discuss?

⇒ When You Are Not Ok with the Appointment

> Sorry, I can't make it then.

> I'd love to, but I really can't.

> Sorry, I'm already tied up until two.

> I'm afraid I've got another meeting then.

> I am afraid I have another appointment then.

> I'm afraid we'll need to find another schedule.

> I'm afraid I can't meet them at ten next Monday.

> I'm afraid I can't make it next Friday. Why don't we put it off sometime next week?

> Unfortunately, I will be on a trip from January 3 to 8, so I couldn't make it then. Although, in the upcoming week, it will be a pleasure to meet with you.

⇒ When You Are Ok with the Appointment

In Speaking

💬 So, that's Monday at 10 AM.

💬 Yes, that's fine. See you then.

💬 Sounds Ok to me. Let's do that.

💬 Perfect, see you on Monday at 10.

💬 All right. I'll see you on Monday at 5:30.

💬 I look forward to seeing you on Tuesday.

💬 Well, this schedule suits me. Let's do that.

💬 I am looking forward to hearing from you.

💬 Excellent. I look forward to meeting you then.

💬 Perfect. I very much look forward to talking with you.

💬 That sounds sensible. So, I'll see you on Monday at 2.

💬 Yes, that would be fine. Let's say it's settled. See you then.

💬 All right, that's perfect for me. I look forward to meeting you.

💬 Yes, next week works fine. Shall we plan it at two on Monday?

> That would be just fine. I can't wait to meet you. See you on Monday.

> Just to confirm the schedule of our meeting: Tuesday 10 July at 10 AM.

In Writing

📄 Dear ...,

Again, thank you for the email. I want to confirm my participation to the kickoff meeting on Friday, May 5, at the New York offices. If possible, I would like to have the risk analysis notes to get a head start.

Yours truly,

📄 Dear ...,

This is to confirm my participation at the Review meeting on Monday, November 25, from 11:30 am to 1:00 pm UTC.

Thanks for sharing all the necessary documentation ahead of the meeting; this is appreciated.

Kindly book me a room in the same hotel and a rental car for in-city transportation.

Thanks for your world-class assistance,

Oliver

📄 Dear ...,

I am writing to confirm the meeting made over the phone yesterday. We agreed to meet at the Novotel Paris Centre on Thursday, June 7, at 10 am.

Please contact me at +33 xx-xxxxx or reply to this mail if there is any change of time or location. Feel free to call my assistant or me if you have any questions.

ENGLISH FOR MEETINGS

I look forward to meeting you.

Yours truly,

📄 Dear ...,

This is a gentle reminder to confirm your meeting with Eliyahu Goldman tomorrow January 22nd, by 11 am. He will meet you at your office.

Kindly reach out to me for any useful accommodation.

Thank you, and have a fruitful meeting.

Respectfully,

⇒ Put off or Cancel

💬 I'm afraid our meeting is conflicting with another appointment I didn't consider. If you don't mind, I propose that we put it off. What about next Thursday at two?

💬 Could we put off our tomorrow meeting for I am not feeling good these days? I will need to rest tomorrow, as my doctor recommended. But if you don't mind, I am up for next Wednesday at nine at the same place.

💬 I am sorry to inform you that we will not be able to meet tomorrow. I got a last-minute change in a committee session. Please let me know if next Monday at ten will suit you. Otherwise, tell me when we could reschedule the rendezvous.

💬 An unexpected event just occurred, and as a result, I have to cancel our appointment. I know it's short notice and I'm sorry about that. I can't seem to find any spot in the coming days. But call me next week so that we can work something out.

⇒ Apologies

💬 I'm afraid I have an impediment that prevents me from attending the meeting. Just to inform you and present apologies.

💬 I'm afraid I've got an important and urgent engagement to handle. I will not be able to take part in the meeting. Wishing you a fruitful workshop.

💬 Unfortunately, I will not be able to attend the review meeting as a result of unforeseen events that cropped up. I am looking forward to reading the minutes to keep up with you. Have a productive and fruitful meeting.

💬 I'm afraid I have a critical project that is running late and needs my full attention. Hence, I will not be able to attend tomorrow's meeting. If you need any documentation from me, kindly let me know. Have a good day.

⇒ Follow Up

💬 My assistant will let you know the schedule of the meeting.

💬 My assistant will also be joining us. She will get in touch with you for all the details.

💬 I will have my assistant send you an email to let you know the time and place of our appointment.

💬 I will have my PA send you an email to let you know where our meeting will be held. She will also send you the agenda I'd like to discuss.

3. Open

⇒ **Short Expressions to Open**

💬 Good afternoon and welcome to this meeting. I will keep it as brief as possible since we are all busy these days. Can we make a start?

💬 Thanks for attending this important meeting. The discussions will be necessary to define a clear path for the new policy implementation. As all participants have received the documentation, let's go around the table to allow everyone to introduce himself.

💬 Good evening. Thanks for taking the time to have this meeting. We have called it to examine the business proposal of an information security startup. Let's go around the table for participants to introduce themselves. As everyone is here, let's begin.

💬 Good morning. Thanks for coming. We have a lot of ground to cover, so let's get started. Before going any further, I am pleased to introduce a new consultant, Mrs. Lynda Prayat. She will be working with the healthcare team. Welcome on board, Lynda! I wish you all the best in this new assignment. You have the floor.

💬 Thanks to all of you. We have a tight schedule today, so we'll need to cut corners. Let's get the ball rolling. But before, I have the privilege to introduce the new Digital Director, Mr. McMillan. He has a very long list of accomplishments in the sector, and many of us already met him on different occasions. Mr. McMillan, welcome on board! The floor is yours.

⇒ Informal Meeting at a Restaurant

Greetings

💬 Hello David, it's good to see you again.

Welcome to Hong Kong.

Thanks for arranging this informal meeting.

I hope you made a safe trip.

Did you have any trouble finding the place?

Did you find your way with no trouble?

Are you familiar with the area?

💬 Good afternoon Kim, it's always a pleasure meeting with you.

Thanks for taking the time to have this informal meeting.

I hope you made a safe commute.

Did you get the correct indications from the assistant?

How about your colleague Christopher at the Boston office?

💬 Hello Abdel, how have you been?

How is the family?

How about the traffic?

This restaurant is charming.

Thanks for taking the lead to have this meeting.

I hope you made safe travel.

Are you familiar with the area?

Which hotel are you staying?

How about your colleague Adams at the Boston office?

Did you get good indications from the assistant?

Opening discussion (consulting request)

- What are you up to?
- Are you hitting the buffers?
- What can you tell me about your product?
- Where do you stand in your new software project?
- What is at the top of your agenda for this meeting?
- Are you also consulting with our so-called all-time competitors on other projects?
- It's in the air that your food-processing branch distribution system is facing aggressive competition.
- Are there specific objectives that the CEO of your firm wants to meet, and what is the dedicated timeframe on his agenda?

Opening discussion (job request)

- Can you walk us through your CV?
- Can you tell me a bit about yourself?
- What do you know about our clients?
- What do you know about our market?
- What do you know about our products?
- How many cars were sold globally last year?

- 💬 Are you good at solving big hairy problems?
- 💬 What are some of your sectorial competences?
- 💬 Tell me about a time you changed someone's mind.
- 💬 What are your most robust functional competences?
- 💬 Can you tell me why you are interested in this position?
- 💬 Can you tell me about a significant personal achievement?
- 💬 "What important truth do very few people agree with you?" (3)
- 💬 Did you ever break the rules, and what are some of the cases?
- 💬 Are you well versed in financial legislation as required for the position?
- 💬 Give a case where you had an issue with your boss and the way it wound up.
- 💬 Are you good at managing teams remotely and handling multiple projects?
- 💬 What is the biggest project problem you have solved, and how you made it?
- 💬 What is your unique selling proposition for this position, or why should we hire you?
- 💬 Will you make it in the tech industry, and how are you planning to hit the ground running?
- 💬 Is there any particular reason why you are interested in changing companies at this moment?
- 💬 What means risk management for you, and can you give me a case where you mitigated a serious risk?

⇒ Formal Meetings

Greetings

- Hi everyone, welcome to this meeting.

- Dear participants, welcome to the 2nd review meeting of the year.

- Ladies and gentlemen welcome to the 2nd annual review meeting of the Southern American region's portfolio.

- Dear officials, representatives, investors, lenders, partners, managers, recipients, and actors welcome to this meeting.

Absence

- We have apologies from many stakeholders for today's meeting.

- Unfortunately, many are not able to make it today due to tight conflicting agendas.

- At least three persons are going to miss out on today's meeting due to conflicting schedules.

Context

- **Since** the last gathering, quite a few milestones have been covered.

- We have covered a pretty large amount of ground **since** the last review.

- **Since** the previous meeting, teams have worked hard, along with challenging changes in the environment.

- **During 2018,** we have initiated several organizational adjustments to enhance our ability to achieve better outcomes for our clients, and to strengthen our expertise and footprint on corporate strategy issues.

- **Following a year during which** we registered our weakest revenues performance of the past five years, sales growth is expected to slightly recover in 2019. However, the market is confronted by numerous risks, including exchange rates, financial stress, and geopolitical concerns.

💬 **By the end of this year**, it is estimated that a new regulation will be adopted by the Congress regarding food, beverage, and supplement labeling as well as ingredient review.

Objective / Agenda

💬 The task at the top of our agenda is the review of performance.

💬 We are here today because our new drug failed to get FDA approval.

💬 The main objective of the meeting is to go over the new risk mitigation plan.

💬 We'll be going through the report of the telecommunication authority, which is pretty bad.

💬 We'll be discussing the terms of reference for the upcoming international symposium in Italy.

💬 We'll be looking at the staff turnaround plan and discussing scenarios for overheads optimization.

💬 The objective of the meeting is to prepare the due diligence for the airline client's acquisition of *Fly the World*.

💬 The board had advanced the schedule for new projects' approval, so we will be working on nailing down all projects in the pipeline.

Box: 5 Rules to Be an Effective Team Player

1. Add value in meetings by getting your points across intelligently.

2. Make constructive criticism and help others also to get their points across.

ENGLISH FOR MEETINGS

3. Do your homework ahead of meetings by preparing your points along with relevant research.

4. Know your role in the meeting and play to that: support, evaluation, presentation, moderation, advice, or technical.

5. Listen actively, take notes, and show interest by closing your laptop and locking your smartphone.

4. Agree

exactly/ absolutely/ definitely	we are on the same page/ I adhere to	I fully agree with you/ of course/ sure	I couldn't agree more/ I perfectly agree
we are on the same wavelength	you took the words right out of my mouth	I couldn't say it any better	why not?/ agreed/ I have no objection
nothing to say/ why not?	no doubt/ in the same vein/ furthermore	I share your point of view	this is also my point of view
I approve/ I also think that	I suppose so/ I guess so	I quite agree/ I totally agree/ I truly agree	I will just add that/ that's right
just to complete/ I also confirm	we agree with you/ we totally agree with	we acknowledge and agree that	we see eye to eye/ that's a good point

💬 I suppose so.

💬 Exactly. That's true.

💬 We are on the same page.

💬 I fully agree with you.

ENGLISH FOR MEETINGS

- 💬 I couldn't say it any better.
- 💬 I totally agree with Roberto.
- 💬 I share your point of view.
- 💬 This is also my point of view.
- 💬 Why not? I have no objection.
- 💬 We are on the same wavelength.
- 💬 I couldn't agree more on this point.
- 💬 No doubt, this proposition is the best.
- 💬 I also think that this is the right thing to do.
- 💬 You took the words right out of my mouth.
- 💬 I think we are now on the same wavelength.
- 💬 I will just add that we will even save more money.
- 💬 Feel free to agree or disagree and express your views.
- 💬 I also think that this level of overspending is a big issue.
- 💬 I also confirm that the project wasn't adequately funded.
- 💬 I am OK if you say that the vendor is competent for the job.
- 💬 In the same vein, I strongly agree with the low-cost proposition.
- 💬 I hope you agree with me that this is not the case for that client.
- 💬 The board will adhere to the restructuring plan if we present a forecasted scorecard.
- 💬 I fully agree with you that there is a need to strengthen the existing covenant provisions.
- 💬 I agree with Mrs. Aditya on this point that setting a high anchor price will help secure a better deal.

- **We acknowledge and agree that** we have not entered a contractual relationship with the supplier regarding such a bundle offer.

- **We agree with you**, Mr. Chairman, **and with you**, Mr. Director, that the firm, and more particularly the IT department, can enhance its capacity to handle the software configuration.

5. Disagree

I'm afraid I don't agree with	I tend to disagree with	you may not even agree with me	I don't share your point of view
forget it/ you must be joking	I take your point/ it's too risky	I don't think it's a good idea	I don't know/ it's a long shot
I strongly disagree	absolutely not/ of course not	nothing of the kind	sorry, but .../ excuse me, but ...
there is a problem with	it's looks good on paper, but ...	I am not sure I agree with you	It's true, but ...

❞ I don't know.

❞ It's a long shot.

❞ I take your point.

❞ I strongly disagree.

❞ Sorry, but it is too risky.

❞ I don't think it's a good idea.

❞ I don't share your point of view.

❞ I'm afraid I don't agree with you.

ENGLISH FOR MEETINGS

- No, I mean **nothing of the kind**.

- **There is a problem with** your point.

- **I tend to disagree with** this approach.

- **I am not sure I agree with** your analysis.

- **You may not even agree with** me on this.

- **To be honest, I don't think it's a good idea.**

- **It's true, but** only for one region out five regions surveyed.

- **It's looks good on paper, but** almost impossible to realize.

- **I'm afraid** this strategy will reveal some of our weaknesses.

- **I tend to disagree** with any kind of ill-informed decision-making.

- **Of course not,** we are not saying that your team is not competent.

- **You may not even agree with me,** but this little app is the solution.

- **It looks good on paper, but** it's going to be an uphill battle to execute.

- **I strongly disagree** with the proposition to force the hand of the union.

- **I'm afraid I don't agree** with you on the composition of the negotiating team.

- **I am not sure I agree with you** on this work plan, especially on the first-round activities.

- **I don't think it is a good idea to** target 4% market share in only a three-year time frame.

- **It is too risky** to put all the eggs in one basket, especially when it comes to Forex trading.

- **There is a problem with** this proposition because we don't have the results of the survey yet.

- **This option is a long shot** because it is unlikely that you will educate people to create a market for your product.

ENGLISH FOR MEETINGS

6. Interrupt

sorry for interrupting you, but ...	let's get back on track	I apologize for interrupting, but ...	I'm afraid I have to interrupt you
we'll take that up later	we'll come back to you in a second	you will get a spot to share your view	you will have the opportunity to react
can I just interrupt you here?	can we go back to ...	please, let's hear what [...] has to say	could I finish please?
let's close this parenthesis	let's hit a pause	hold on a moment please	can I come in here?
if I could just come in here	could I just say something about that?	just a second please, we'll get back to you.	let's get down to business

99 Let's get back on track.

99 If I could just come in here?

99 Can I just interrupt you here?

99 Could I finish, please? Thank you.

99 We'll come back to you in a second.

ENGLISH FOR MEETINGS

- 💬 Please, can we **go back to the point?**

- 💬 **Could I just say** something about that?

- 💬 Just a **second,** please. We'll **get back** to you.

- 💬 Please, **let's hear what Mrs. Sullivan has to say.**

- 💬 **Let's** close this parenthesis and get back to the issue.

- 💬 **You will get a spot to speak** in a minute. Thank you.

- 💬 **Let's hit a pause.** We will get back after the coffee break.

- 💬 **Sorry for interrupting you,** but we must **get back on track.**

- 💬 **Hold** on a moment please, you will have a spot very soon.

- 💬 **I apologize for interrupting,** but we just need to know if there is a solution.

- 💬 Please, in a moment, **you will have the opportunity to share your views.** Thanks for your understanding.

- 💬 **I'm afraid I have to interrupt you** because the question is whether or not we can outsource the customer service and what the cost will be.

7. Ask Opinion

can you share your view about ...?	can you give your take on ..?	what's your opinion (advice) about ...?	do you think this idea has legs?
how do you anticipate ...?	how are you envisioning ...?	what do you think about ...?	would you like to share your opinion?
do you have any objection on ...?	can you share your thoughts on ...?	could you weigh in with your arguments?	how serious do you think it is?

💬 How do you anticipate it?

💬 How are you envisioning it?

💬 What do you think about it?

💬 Do you have any objection?

💬 How serious do you think it is?

💬 Do you think this idea has legs?

💬 Can you share your thoughts please?

💬 Would you like to share your opinion?

💬 Could you weigh in with your arguments?

💬 What's your advice on the sales targets?

- **Can you give your take** on this proposition?
- **Do you think** it will work in the Asian region?
- How important **do you think** the damages are?
- **How are you envisioning** the physical relocation of the factory?
- **What do you think about** the acquisition in terms of synergies?
- **How do you anticipate** problems in the delivery of a building permit?
- **Can you share your thoughts** on the performance of robots in your plant?
- **Do you have any objection** to the new management remuneration proposition?
- **Do you think it's a good idea** to link partners' remuneration to the performance of the fund?
- **Would you like to share your opinion** on the integration of the siloed systems into a unique platform?

8. Clarify

do you mean that ...?	are you saying that ...?	is your point that ...?	what I meant to say was ...
that's not what I meant	I was trying to say that ...	I'm afraid I didn't get you	it's worth mentioning that
can you put it in layman terms	it is important to mention that ...	the rationale of ... is that ...	there is a little misunderstanding here
I don't think you understood me well	I just want to highlight some of ...	It would be good to clarify that ...	don't get me wrong, I didn't say that

💬 That's not what I meant.

💬 I'm afraid I didn't get you.

💬 I think you heard me wrong.

💬 Don't get me wrong. I didn't say that.

💬 I don't think you understood me well.

💬 There is a little misunderstanding here.

💬 Are you saying that the prototype is not fully functional?

💬 There's a persistent misunderstanding about outsourcing.

💬 Is your point that the product launch should be postponed?

- **Would you like to explain** the agile meetings concept briefly?

- **I don't think you've well understood** the point of Mrs. Lopez.

- **I'm not sure I understand** you when saying fixed costs will vary.

- **I just want to highlight** the fact that costs will outweigh the benefits.

- **What I meant to say was** we must first focus on low hanging fruits.

- **Do you mean that** sales will decline as a result of the new legislation?

- Please, **can you put it in layman terms** so that everyone can follow up?

- **What I meant to say was** if there is no competition, there is no market.

- **I just want to highlight some of** the possibilities available in the short term.

- **I just wanted to highlight some** updates just in case it got buried in your mails.

- **I was trying to say that** over-communication is better than under-communication.

- **It would be good to clarify what** sunk costs are and that they are not considered in the net present value of the project.

- **It is important to mention that** partnership and proprietorship forms are not suitable for a startup expecting to raise funds and be sold in the future.

- **The rationale of** the $20 billion market size **is that** if a startup is successful and able to capture 5% of the market, then it could reach an income target of $1 billion per year.

9. Make a Point

here's the deal	the point is	I'd like to make a point here	if I could just add a point
I'd like to make a contribution	I'd like to draw your attention on	I'd like to warn you against	I want to emphasize that
I'd like to react to ...	I'd like to highlight that	I'd like to add that ...	I want to underscore that
in the same vein/ in the same way	just to make a small contribution...	I want to comment on ...	could I draw your attention to ...
could I come here?	can I make a point on ...?	can I just comment on ...?	could I bring a point on ...?

> **I'd like to comment** on the product-market fit.

> **The point is** that it's not the hard part of the job.

> **Could I just add a point here** about the cost centers?

> **Can I make a point here** about Mr. Riley's intervention?

> This story **makes very good points** about people. Don't you agree?

> **Can I come here** to talk about the adoption strategy of the product?

- 💬 **I would like to make a point** about the positioning of the company.
- 💬 **The point is** the negotiation is much more complicated than expected.
- 💬 **If I could just add a point,** I want to explain the tests and measurements.
- 💬 **I want to emphasize that** the team must sign a non-disclosure agreement.
- 💬 **I'd like to shed light on** the conclusions of the team on the market validation.
- 💬 **I'd like to warn you against** the possible retaliation from foreign governments.
- 💬 **I'd like to draw your attention to** the software's end-user configuration requirements.
- 💬 **I would like to react to** Alan's presentation of the MVP (minimum viable product).
- 💬 **Here's the deal**: the client moved up the deadline, so I need to see the draft as soon as possible.
- 💬 **In the same vein,** I want to add that the results of the customer survey are satisfactory if not perfect.
- 💬 **In the same vein,** higher customer service will also impact sales positively in the medium term.
- 💬 **Just to make a small contribution,** I'd like to say that the accuracy of the disbursement rate must be verified.

10. Give a Reason

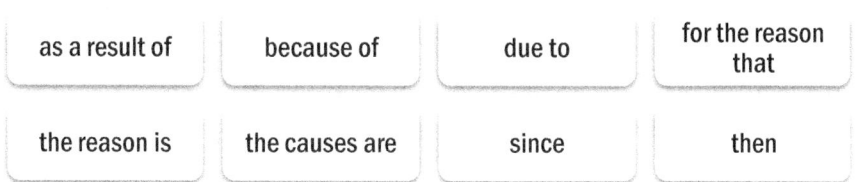

| as a result of | because of | due to | for the reason that |

| the reason is | the causes are | since | then |

- The budget overrun is **due to** poor general expenses forecasts.
- Higher margins, **as a result of** reduced prime costs may be expected.
- We are looking for a new designer **because** the current one is resigning.
- The region is still depressed **because of** criminality and low public investments.
- The new prototype seems to be a success **since** we got past all the preliminary tests.
- Costs are down here **for the reason** that the turnaround has reduced overhead expenses.
- **As a result of** the marketing campaign, revenue, and gross margin are higher than forecasted.

- The excellent usage rate of solar pumps is **due to** the massive implication of stakeholders.

- The services that we provide may become temporarily unavailable **as a result of** a system malfunction.

- We have not renewed the contract with the vendor. **The reason was** we were unhappy with their performance.

- Our customer base has grown by 6,500 in size between 2015 and 2017 **as a result of** higher market penetration.

- The conference was attended by a large public **as a result of** the excellent communication done by the PR department.

- Staff turnover, lack of funding, and burnout **are** some of **the primary causes** of the project's failure following implementation.

- On the Fintech Project, we need people with scientific backgrounds **because** it makes it much easier for the team to talk to one another.

11. Report Progress

- We were afraid the deal was lost, but our negotiation team **pulled a rabbit out of his hat** to get an agreement.

- We started this project on a shoestring, but the teams worked really hard **to scale it up into** a sizeable profitable venture.

- Months after searching how to boost declining market share, our company can now **get** an offensive strategy **off the ground**.

- Starting out in the grain business in 2011, our London-based subsidiary **had gradually expanded** into the food-processing industry.

- Since its inception in 2012 as a small development organization with a dozen employees in Bangalore, Water Project **had grown into** an internationally recognized, nonprofit social enterprise.

12. Report Regress

- Profits **have been declining over** the past three years.
- Local sales **have been declining over** the past two years.
- I am not responsible for the **mess**; you need to look somewhere else.
- The project **is going down in flames** due to siloed platforms failing to integrate.
- The new product launch **wasn't successful**, so all the hard work **went down the drain**.
- What can we do the reverse this trend of **declining profitability** in the premium market?
- In the last quarter, the **profits were 15% lower than** the same quarter three years earlier.
- Despite offering a high-end product, the company **fails to capture a fair share** of the premium market.
- The project on health care **wasn't approved** by the committee, so we have to go **back to the drawing board**.
- Unfortunately, the new tech venture **is not going to fly** due to **severe technical issues** to fill its central promise profitably.
- I don't want to **add fuel to the fire**, but the IT project **is also suffering** from the poor asset management of the administration team.
- Despite their unique brand name, the profits **dwindled significantly over** the past three years, and specifically in the previous quarter, net income **was down** 15% **compared to** last year.

13. Moderate

💬 We can take that up later. Let's focus on the task in hand.

💬 We can take that up next week at the staff meeting. Let's get back to the subject.

💬 So far, we have done a review of last month's activities. Now we are going to make the next month's agenda.

💬 So far, we have gathered insights into the new marketing plan. Now I'd like to hit the next point. Can you present the budgeted sales for next year?

💬 We all agree, to some extent, that ideas are irrelevant if there are not backed up with a minimum of data. Now let's get to the next point. What is the proposed team for the BIONADE engagement?

14. Close

💬 It was a very constructive meeting. Thanks for your participation. I wish you a fruitful day.

💬 Thanks for attending this workshop. The date of the next discussions will be communicated later. The meeting is over. Have a good day!

💬 The next meeting will take place in two weeks. Thanks for your active participation. The workshop is over. I wish you a productive day.

ENGLISH FOR MEETINGS

Case: Internal Meeting Transcript

[Chairman]: Good morning, everyone. I see empty chairs. Please, move closer to fill these places. We are required to make meetings agile, so this is going to be a 30-minute meeting.

Can we make a start? All right. Thank you all for coming despite the short notice. It's great seeing you all attend the meeting. I appreciate it. We didn't meet for four weeks, so there is a pretty large amount of ground to cover. We'll need to cut corners to make it in half an hour, so please be short and concise.

Before going further, let's go around the table to allow old and new participants to get to know each other.

Well, thanks. The proposed agenda is:

1. Apologies
2. Compliance and regulatory matters
3. Due diligence for *Fly The World* acquisition
4. Adoption of the human resource integration plan

Do we have excuses for today's meeting?

[Catherine]: Pierre will come to the meeting late. Mary has informed that she is not going to attend this session. We have also received the apologies of Samantha because she is grappling with the labor union unrest.

[Chairman]: Good. Is there any amendment of agenda that someone would like to suggest?

[David]: Thank you, John (chairman). I'd like to suggest that we put point 3 at the top of the agenda because the discussions will bring clarification for the second point.

[Jerry]: I wonder if it's not better to merge the third point on regulatory matters with the following point on due diligence because there is a redundancy.

[Ayush]: AOB (Any Other Business) is missing; it is useful for discussing miscellaneous issues that will come down the road.

[Chairman]: Ok, sounds good to meet. So, please add to the minutes that the proposed amendments are applied. All right, let's get started.

[Chairman]: David, can you tell us where we stand on the acquisition of *Fly The World*?

[David]: Thanks, John. We had already informed the target that we own more than 15% of voting rights. I will let Jerry walk you through the due diligence checklist.

[Jerry]: Thank you. Here is the nine-point checklist of the due diligence.

- Corporate structure & general matters
- Taxes
- Strategic fit
- Intellectual property
- Material Assets
- Contracts
- Employees and senior management
- Litigation
- Compliance and regulatory matters

We have a couple of issues with taxes, intellectual property, and employees. These issues are related to the fact that a new piece of legislation is allegedly underway. It can hypothetically affect these elements. Otherwise, everything is under control.

[Chairman]: So, we are going to keep tabs on this legislation. We'll take that up next month to see how things are unfolding. Let's hit the next point. Can you present the plan for the integration of both companies' staff after acquisition?

[Jerry]: As the companies are operating in the same industry, the priority will be to cut redundant senior positions. Therefore, C-level management will be drastically downsized for these positions will be attributed to the parent company's C-level. As a result, we are going to make 17 positions redundant at the C-level. Similarly, the business and operations levels will be trimmed to eliminate overstaffing. At these levels, 158 jobs are on the line. In summary, 175 positions will be stripped away.

[Chairman]: Thanks Jerry, for these efficient answers. I want you to pay close attention to labor unions. You might have to negotiate this plan and leave more jobs on the table. Please, follow this through very carefully and report directly to me. Don't surprise me because I hate surprises.

Do we have any other business?

...

Well, the next meeting will take place in two weeks. Thanks for your active participation. The meeting is over. I wish you a fruitful day.

15. Exercises

1. How would you call the meetings with the below information, in speaking and in writing?
    a. Date: Monday, January 20th 2020; time: 10 AM; place: Palace Restaurant; object: discuss a contract.
    b. Date: next week; time: 2 PM; place: office; object: prepare a mission.

2. Which are the five expressions used when you agree with someone?
    a. We are on the same page
    b. Sorry for interrupting you, but
    c. I quite agree
    d. Is your point that ...?
    e. I agree with you
    f. I couldn't say it any better
    g. I'd like to react to
    h. I take your point
    i. It is important to mention that
    j. We are on the same wavelength
    k. I tend to disagree with you

3. Which are the three expressions that are not used to make a point?
    a. I'd like to make a point here
    b. Could I finish please?
    c. If I could just add a point
    d. I take your point
    e. I'd like to make a contribution
    f. I'd like to draw your attention on
    g. I'd like to warn you about
    h. I'm afraid I don't agree with you
    i. I want to emphasize that

This page is intentionally left blank.

About the Author

My name is Adama Komou. I have worked for a couple of small and medium-sized consulting firms. I currently work at the World Bank. My field of competence cuts across start-ups, business development, project management, and finance.

I am currently completing a Master of Science in Finance and Investment at the London School of Business and Finance. I hold a bachelor's degree in Economics from the University Ouaga II.

I'd love to read your reviews for this endeavor to help me figure out how relevant it was. You can send your feedback directly to me at the email address below.

I will be delighted to make your acquaintance.

Yours truly,
Adama Komou
Email: adama_komou@yahoo.fr

ABOUT THE AUTHOR

This page is intentionally left blank.

Bibliography

1. **Haroun, Chris.** *Networking to Get Customers, a Job or Anything You Want.* s.l. : Haroun Education Ventures Inc., 2017.

2. **Andler, Nicolai.** *Tools for Project Management, Workshops and Consulting.* s.l. : Publicis, 2011. ISBN 978-3-89578-671-6.

3. **Thiel, Peter.** *Zero to One: Notes on Startups, or How to Build the Future.* New York : Crown Publishing Group, 2014. ISBN: 978-0-8041-3929-8.

Printed in Great Britain
by Amazon